POEMS

گزیدهٔ شعر

Reza Mohammadi

POEMS

گزیدۀ شعر

First published in 2012
by The Poetry Translation Centre Ltd
PO Box 61051
London SE16 4YY

www.poetrytranslation.org

Poems © Reza Mohammadi, 2012

Translations from the Dari © Nick Laird and Hamid Kabir
Introduction © Hamid Kabir

ISBN: 978-0-9560576-9-3

The Poetry Translation Centre gratefully acknowledges the
financial support of Arts Council England.

British Library Cataloguing-in-Publication Data.
A catalogue record for this book is available from the British Library.

Designed in Albertina by Libanus Press
Printed in the UK by Imprint Digital

Contents

Introduction   6

Drawing   9

Irony   13

Letter to the Rain   15

The Word   17

To Love   19

Providence   21

The Football   23

The Wind   25

Illegal Immigrant   27

Friendship   29

Introduction

Reza Mohammadi is an Afghan journalist, critic and poet, whose three collections of poetry have won many prizes for his poetry in Persian-speaking countries. He is the winner of prizes for the best poem published in 1996 and 1997 in Iran, the most influential Afghan poet in Iran in 2002, and the poet of the year in Afghanistan in 2004. He has also published articles and commentary in English in *The Guardian*.

Reza was born on 31st December 1979 in Afghanistan's Kandahar province, and his family migrated to Iran when he was four years old. Perhaps this early separation from his homeland nourished his love for Afghanistan. Reza was an excellent student, and read the Quran and classical Arabic from an early age, and specialised in Philosophy and Globalisation in his higher education. His poetry displays such mastery of a broad array of subjects, and his versatility shows itself also in technique: whilst he is better known for his free verse, he has also written numerous popular ghazals and in other classical forms. His poem 'The Voice', also known as 'Drawing', is a classically metered narrative (and Reza's most spoken-about poem) in which he questions the relationship between the creator and the created, and the power and the submission that such a relationship entails. In Reza's work, the reader often finds descriptions of a struggle, a separation from homeland or of a country ravaged by war, and yet there is also a subtle optimism. In 'The Football', for example, Reza writes about the intractability of politics, and yet it should be noted that the youths are also playing a game of football, are also living and enjoying life in the midst of war, and with scant regard to geographic and political boundaries. Likewise, in 'Illegal Immigrant,' there is a moment of pride and pleasure among the difficulties for the stowaway, who crosses the border strapped to the bottom of a truck and 'moment by moment' is 'entering / with glory England.'

Reza's work is distinctive for his thorough knowledge of classical Afghan and Persian writing. His ability to write the beautiful language of poetry is matched by a deep and compassionate knowledge of the Persian region and culture. And though well-versed in politics, art, philosophy, history, he is also a poet wise about domestic, inner tensions, about love, about friendship. He is not a poet whose work is rarefied or separate in its concerns: his poetry reminds people of profound and shared values rather than dividing differences, and it is for this reason that his work has earned him respect amongst all ethnic groups of Afghanistan, Iran and Tajikistan. He is seen as a uniting writer.

HAMID KABIR

رسم

صدا، ز کالبد تن به در کشید مرا
صدا به شکل کسی شد به بر کشید مرا

صدا شد اسپ ستم روح من کشان ز پی‌اش
به خاک بست، به کوه وُ کمر کشید مرا

چه وهم داشت که از ابتدای خلقت من
غریب و کج‌قلق و دربه‌در کشید مرا؟

دو نیمه کرد مرا، پس تو را کشید از من
پس از کنار تو این سویتر کشید مرا

میان ما دری از مرگ کرد نقاشی
به میخ کوفته در پشتِ در کشید مرا

خوشش نیامد این نقش را به هم زد وُ بعد
دگر کشید تو را وُ دگر کشید مرا

من وُ تو را دو پرنده کشید در دو قفس
خوشش نیامد بی‌بال وُ پَر کشید مرا

خوشش نیامد ـ تصویر را به هم زد ـ بعد
پدر کشید تو را وُ پسر کشید مرا

DRAWING

There was a voice and it coursed
from a pair of parched lips,
drawing me out of my body.

The voice was despotic, uncurbed
as a horse dragging my soul
across rocks and up scree.

I don't know why the voice,
the maker, drew me as unroofed,
as a vagrant, a fool,

or why it split me in two
and then drew me from you,
sliding the earth in between us.

It sketched a door of death then
and depicted me nailed to the door –
but that wasn't enough so it rubbed us out

and started from the beginning,
drawing us in the likeness of doves,
caged in separate cages.

It wasn't enough
so it drew me with neither wings nor feathers
but it wasn't enough

so it dashed us to pieces
and drew me as your son, you as my father,
and a moment later I was a stone

رها شدیم تو ماهی شدی و من سنگی
نظاره‌ی تو به خون جگر کشید مرا

خوشش نیامد؛ این بار از تو دشتی ساخت
به خاطر تو نسیم سحر کشید مرا

خوشش نیامد، خط، خط، خط زد این‌ها را
یک استکان چای از خیر و شر کشید مرا

تو را شکر کرد و در دهان من حل کرد
سپس به سمت لبش برد وُ سر کشید مرا

and you were a star shining down on me,
making me into the most precious thing…
It wasn't enough.

It drew you as a desert and me as a breeze
on the long wander through you.
It wasn't enough. It erased us

and sketched me as a cup of tea,
full of good and full of evil,
and made you the sugar that sank in me

and got dissolved and finally we
were lifted up to a pair of parched lips
and drank

زندگی در آیینه

تو گل های مصنوعی
را در گلدان بدلی نقره
کنار پنجره ای تقلبی می مانی
آفتاب مصنوعی
لبخند مصنوعی ات را
تلخ تر می کند

زیبایی صورت مصنوعی ات را روی سینه ام می گذاری
و من با قلب واقعی ام
دوستت دارم

IRONY

You put artificial flowers in a silver-looking vase
beside a painting of a window,
and the sun revealed your smile as fake,

so you rested the mask of your beautiful face
on my chest – but hey, I love you, it's true,
and I love you with all of my heart.

نامه ای به باران

باران سلام

فصل زمستان تمام شد

فصل بهار نیز

کم کم به روز های سر انجام می رسد

از دوری تو سخت ملولند اهل باغ

کی فصل دوری تو به اتمام می رسد؟

باران سلام

باران باران باران

باران مهربان باران بی وفا

باغ عزیز ما را هر کس رسیده از بغلش خاک ریخته است

هر وقت باد آمده از کوه ، دشت،جنگل،

از چارسوی عالم، بر روی باغ ما خس و خاشاک ریخته است

باران باران نازنین

عصر آخرین پرنده این باغ می رود

این راهی ، این مسافر بالای ابر ها ، این قاصد بهار پرستوست

این نامه را به بال پرستو نوشته ام

این نامه می رسد به تو یا نه

کوکب تمام روز برای تو گریه کرد

این نامه را برای دل او نوشته ام

باران باران باران ما

نامه اگر رسید به تو زودتر بیا

LETTER TO THE RAIN

Dear rain,
Winter has passed
and even the spring approaches her end.
You are badly missed in the garden.
When will your absence be over?

Oh Rain! Rain! Rain!
Kind and cold-hearted rain!
It gets nothing, the garden, but dust, red dust,
off the feet of by-passers or blown in by the wind
from deserts and mountains and forests.
Dust piles up by the walls, in the corners.

Rain! Soft rain!
The last bird of the garden will leave after sundown
and I've written this poem on her outstretched wing.
Will it reach you or not?

All day the dahlias cried for you,
and I wrote this for their comfort.

Rain, come at once, come once you get this.

کلمه

کلمه ی متروکی بودم من
در کتابی کهنه
کلمه ی فراموش شده بودم
از عشق از سیاست از دنیا
شاعران از من می گریختند
حروفم از من متنفر بودند
به کلمات دیگر می رفتند و باز نمی گشتند
کلمه ای تنها بودم
بی حرفی
تنها صدای قرن هابا من بود
صدای بردگان
صدای مردگان
صدای جهات دوار زمان

تو آمدی با لب های خونینت
باانگشتان غمگینت
تو آمدی و مرا پیدا کردی
و تمام جهان از من پرشد

THE WORD

I was a word abandoned in an old battered book,
a word forgot by politics, by love and the speaking world.

The poets fled from me. All of my letters detested me,
deserting me for other words without once looking back.

Just like that I was alone, a ghost-word that lacked its letters,
lonely and only the terrible sound of the frenzied centuries

for company, only the sound of the slaves, of the dead,
of the arrows of time flying and flying and flying.

You (o my true love) came with your fierce mouth
and hands of ten desolate fingers and found me,

and the whole world did shout me

...و اما عشق

با هم بر نمی خیزیم
من با اتاق های بندری متروکه در کناره دریا بر می خیزم
تو با باز کردن پنجره اتاق خواب خودت

تو چای دم شده میخوری
من قلبم را چسب زخم می زنم

روز تو خیابانی است که به خیابانی دیگر که به ساختمانی و بعد به خیابانی در شهر خطوط می انجامد
روز من دالانی که از رگهایم می گذرد و با دکمه هایی مسی بسته می شود

به خانه بر می گردیم
تو لباس ارغوانی ات را می پوشی تا ساعت رنگ ها را تنظیم کنی
من پتوی افغانی ام را
برای چای سبز چه وقت خوبی است!

غذا ما را
تلویزیون ،کامپیوتر، اخبار ما را یکی می کند

دوستت دارم چون
آتشی که بخاریش را
دوستم داری چون بخاریی که هیزم را

همدیگر را گرم بغل می کنیم
و هر یک برای خودمان خواب می بینیم

TO LOVE

We don't wake together. I come to
in an empty room by the sea long after
you've woken and opened the window
and showered and dressed and left.

Your day is a street which leads
to a road that reaches a building,
then leads to an avenue, lastly,
caught in the grid of the city.

My day is a corridor that runs
through my veins and is closed
neatly with copper buttons.
We make our own ways home.

You wear your purple dress
to match the colour of the clocks
and I slip on my patu.
A good time for green tea.

Meals bring each together,
as does the TV, the news, the computer.
I love you like the fire loves the stove.
You love me like the stove loves firewood.

Later on we clutch each other and dream our separate dreams.

قضا

بارانی بی وقتم
که خیابان ها درکم نمی کنند

زمان گذشته دورم
که ارواح سیاحان گمنام و ملاحان نامدار
که ارواح همه گذشتگان در من مدفون است

کلمه ای مطرودم
که کودکان از من می گریزند
وشاعران ترکم کرده اند

صورت کنده بتی در بامیانم
که کشتی کشتی کشتی
از وطنم دست به دست
دزدیده می شوم

شغالی مرده ام
در خیابان های لندن
که ازیاد شهرداری رفته ام

PROVIDENCE

I am a rain that nobody wants.
Even the streets don't understand me.
I am the past perfect tense

and deep down inside me are buried
the ghosts of anonymous travellers,
of infamous seadogs and all of the dead.

I am a certain word small children fear
and which the poets have forgotten.
I'm Buddha's face in Bamiyan, stolen

and sold on from my homeland,
and I am a corpse, knocked down
in Stockwell, ignored by the binmen.

فوتبال

سیاست رودخانه بزرگی است
که قریه های ما را از هم جدا می کند

هی سربازان!
تفنگ هایتان را جمع کنید
بی سیم هایتان را ببندید
دستبند و هشدار و کمین چه به کار است
ما از شما نیستیم
تنها می خواهیم از رودخانه رد شویم
توپمان آن طرف افتاده است

...سیاست رودخانه غمگینی است

THE FOOTBALL

Politics is a river that divides the villages.
Hey soldiers!
Put down your guns and still your radios.
There is no need for handcuffs,
for warnings, for an ambush.
We are not one of you.
We are not one of them.
We just want to get across and get back our ball.

باد

باد

وقتی لباس بپوشد

باد وقتی آواز بخواند

باد وقتی کفش های چرمی

وکلاه ابریشمی بپوشد

باد

وقتی که نیمه شب به خانه ام بیاید

با یک دیگ سوپ جو

وقتی در اجتماع

در بین دوستانم می آید

بی شرم لب هایم را می بوسد

در اجتماع اهل سیاست از من می خواهد

با او شعری را بر ضد پادشاه بخوانم با فریاد

او را کسی به چشم نمی بیند زیرا باد است

من بی اختیار

نامش را می گویم

می بوسمش

در کوچه هر طرف دنبالش می دوم

من دیوانه نیستم

آری تنها چندیست

با بادی

عاشقانه رفیقم

THE WIND

if the wind dressed up
if the wind called out
if the wind wore leather shoes

if the wind blew into my house
at the dead of night at noon
with a jar of onion soup

sometimes when I'm with friends
she kisses me full on the mouth
or in the political circle dares me
recite a poem that mocks the king

no-one can see her because she's invisible
but I call her name and call her name
and trail her down the street –
been a long time since I fell for the wind

مهاجر قاچاقی

حتمن آفتاب
تازه از ستیغ کوه قد کشیده است
حتمن
ابرها هنوز ابر
باد ها هنوز باد
خانواده ها هنوز خانواده اند

صدای پارتی
صدای رقص و پایکوبی وشکستن پیاله
صدای خنده
هر دقیقه انفجار می کند
مردم است
شادمانی است

من با دلی بزرگ
در
کشتی بزرگ پادشاهی
زیر سرد کامیون
مرز را لمیده ام
لحظه لحظه
با شکوه
وارد خاک انگلیس می شویم

ILLEGAL IMMIGRANT

it is possible
the sun has risen
and over the mountains
the clouds are there still,
that winds are driving
and families arriving
and there is the sound of a party
sound of dancing, chanting,
and glasses smashing,
the laughter exploding
in every minute and people
and happiness and also
me, with my big heart,
in a ship or strapped under
the truck, I am crossing
the border and moment
by moment am entering
with glory England

رفاقت

ما كفش هاي چرمي هم بوديم
وقتي كنار در همراه مي شويم
از خاطرات همدگر آگاه مي شويم

درخاطرات تو گوساله اي ست رومي
پروار گفته هاي خدايان
بروار نقل
پروار دور باطل تاريخ
از زندگي به مرگ
ار سفسطه به عقل
آن گاه
با كلب كلب كلب
با كلبيان رواق رواق آمده به بقل
پس از تو
پادشاهي
كفشي درست كرده
تحفه نموده است به درويشي
من بچه گوزني بودم به كاشغر
در حمله مغول به خراسان سپر شدم
در بلخ كاغذ سبق
در باميان علم
در غزنه زير دست يكي كفشگر شدم
دزدي مرا خريد
تو از زمان كفش شدن
انگار
اندازه مانده اي
درويش ونسل هاي پسين
هر گز ترا نه ديده نه پوشيده اند
تو تازه مانده اي
من
اما

FRIENDSHIP

Two pairs of well-used leather shoes
belonging somehow together,
we sit in the sunlight by the door
and go over each other's past.

You are the afterthought of a Roman calf,
born in the shadows of a goddess's temple,
bred to wisdom and vanity, from life to death
you are grown into the centre of all attention

then a king made two shoes from you and gave you to a monk.

Meanwhile, I was a baby Elk in China.
The Mongols made a shield of me, the Persians
a parchment in Balkh, and in Bamiyan
I acted as a standard all could see.
In Kabul I fell into the hands of a cobbler
before a thief with one eye bought me.

You, from the time you were a pair of shoes,
up to this present moment
have remained essentially the same.
The monk and subsequent generations
neither wore you nor noticed you much.
You're still remarkably fresh

با دزدهاي مختلفي راه رفته ام
دزدان مرا زمان به زمان شب به شب
با خود گرفته اند و به این جا کشیده اند
اینک من و تو آه
همراه همراه همراه
از خاطرات هم دگر آگاه
......
ما کفش هاي چرمي هم هستیم

but I have walked among robbers
day after day and night after night
and they dragged me with them to here

where now we sit by this door in the sun
and forever have known each other,
since we are two pairs of shoes made from leather.